*Sports Action*

# Karate

*Sports Action*
# Karate

Edited by
Dan Bradley

OCTOPUS BOOKS

**Acknowledgements**
Photographs
Cover picture: Mike O'Neil (Octopus
Publishing Group)
S. Himme 126; R. Neukam 78. All others by
A. Bachmüller and W. D. Wichmann

Published in 1989 by
Octopus Books Limited
Michelin House
81 Fulham Road
London SW3 6RB

English Translation
© 1989 Octopus Books Limited

Title of original German edition
*Ritching Karate by Wolf-Dieter Wichmann*
© 1985 BLV Verlagsgesellschaft mbH, Munich

ISBN 0 7064 5006 X

Photoset by
SX Composing Limited
Rayleigh, Essex
Produced by Mandarin Offset
Printed and bound in Hong Kong

# Contents

# *Foreword*

Karate – everyone knows the evocative name of this Far Eastern martial art. There are already a number of books which describe the techniques of karate, and this book is simply an attempt to explain those techniques according to what each is used for, and also to explain how they can be taught and improved. The book is intended to help you understand the co-ordination within karate. There are many small individual steps along the road to full mastery of karate, and each of them has to be not only learned, but perfected until it comes as second nature. But it is the co-ordination and sequences of the individual techniques which are most important, and you can't fully understand karate until you understand the purpose of everything you have learned.

It is often said that karate is simply a type of ballet, but anyone who studies and understands karate will disagree with this statement.

At this point, I have to thank everyone who has accompanied me along my own route towards a mastery of karate and given me so much patient and expert help. My thanks also go to everyone who has given me active support in producing this book. And lastly my good wishes go to you, the reader. I wish you the best of luck in your endeavours.

# Introduction

## What karate is, and what karate isn't

### Karate is
- The Japanese version of the fastest martial art in the world
- A comprehensive route towards physical fitness
- A safe method of self-defence
- An outstanding means towards mental and physical discipline

### Karate is not
- The quickest way to kill someone
- Boxing using your hands and feet
- Smashing planks and bricks with your bare hands
- The best way to get your nose broken.

## Where and how can you learn karate?

### Clubs

The most common way of learning karate is by training in a karate club. The advantages of a club are that it is usually cheap and there is more intensive contact between members.

One disadvantage is that often the teaching is done in large groups of people of mixed abilities, and the person doing the training may not necessarily be the best there is, because there is not normally a great deal of money to be made out of teaching karate in this way.

### Schools

Almost as popular are the karate schools, where teaching karate is done commercially, so it will cost you more. The advantages are that you will be taught with other people of similar ability to your own, in smaller groups (because the rooms they use will probably be smaller) and, as the success of a school depends to a large degree on the reputation of its teachers, they will be better.

One disadvantage is that schools have a fairly high drop-out rate.

### Private coaching

Private coaching is expensive and, because there is little contact with other learners, tends to have a rather theoretical bent to it. There is less incentive to learn when you have no-one else around to compare your performance against. You should only use private coaching when group learning isn't available.

### Teaching yourself

Teaching yourself from books is the hardest method and is almost certainly doomed to failure. The energy you need to get to an advanced stage is much greater than with a teacher.

So teaching yourself is very rarely a good idea, and only in rare cases will you succeed. On the other hand, books are ideal as material to supplement your practical training.

*Group training in a dojo, or karate school*

# The history of karate

## Origins

The origins of karate lie in the distant past. Throughout history the ability to defend yourself has been vitally important, especially in periods when there was nothing resembling the police forces of today. The peoples of Asia, with their tendency to categorise and order even the smallest aspects of everyday life, created a variety of martial arts which allowed them to defend themselves effectively. In China these included Kempo, developed by the monk Daruma (or Bodhidharma as he is known in Japanese) and usually known as Shaolin-Kempo. When large-scale trading began between China and the Japanese island of Okinawa a blend of the two countries' martial arts evolved, which was known as Okinawa-Te (*te* meaning hand; hend 'Okinawa-hand').

Many of the rulers of the time forbade their subjects to carry weapons. During these periods there was always a major upsurge in interest in martial arts which did not use weapons, though these arts still remained secret. Two examples of this are the period around 1429, during the reign of the Emperor Shohashi, and in 1609 after the conquest by Shimazu.

It was not until 1900 that Okinawa-Te was given its first public demonstration, and in 1901 it began to be taught as a sport in schools on Okinawa. Since then it has spread from the warrior castes to ordinary people.

In 1922 Gichin Funakoshi, a professor from Okinawa now regarded as the founder of modern karate, was invited to mainland Japan. He was asked to demonstrate Okinawa-Te or Kara-Te as part of a presentation of ancient Japanese martial arts.

Because Kempo was Chinese the people of Okinawa called it Kara-Te, or China-hand. As well as meaning China, the word also means empty, so Funakoshi changed the meaning of karate to 'empty hand'. His demonstration made such a lasting impression on those who saw it that Funakoshi was asked to stay in Japan and teach karate. He taught in various universities before he founded his own style of karate, Shotokan. Shotokan comprises two words in Japanese. Shoto was the pen name adopted by Funakoshi and Kan means something along the lines of hall, area or meeting.

And thus the martial art of karate became the sport of karate, which allowed people to train without getting hurt and to compete with each other. 1936 was also the first time an official Jiyu-Kumite or sparring match was held; before that date only *kata* competitions had been held, in which participants demonstrate their mastery of technique.

It was only after the Second World War that karate became familiar in the West. It captured the interest of several people who were keen enough to go to Japan to study this fascinating martial art. Within a few years they had imported some

*Training at a karate club*

teachers of karate into Europe and the United States. These teachers opened their own karate schools, often developing their own style variations at the same time.

Parallel development in Europe and the New World led to the inauguration of the first world karate championships, held, of course, in Tokyo in 1970. Japan is still the spiritual home of karate, but the Western countries are gradually catching up and several of them are now ahead of Japan in Sport Kumite (competition fighting).

Karate is traditionally done wearing the Japanese white cotton jacket and trousers, or *gi*. Of course there is no reason why you shouldn't train in the same clothes as you would for any other sport, though part of the technique of karate is the way you look. Also, it is difficult to do some of the fast, snapped-back movements of karate if you aren't wearing the white cotton suit.

The suit shouldn't be too light or it will stick to you when you start perspiring. Nor should it be too heavy, which can restrict your freedom of movement in some of the very rapid movements. For this reason a light judo suit is most suitable for the beginner, whereas people who have reached a more advanced stage tend to prefer a slightly stronger quality.

The belt is also made from cotton and its colour denotes the grade a learner or teacher has reached.

The jacket should come down to your buttocks. The trousers should be ankle-length; sometimes they are shorter, but they shouldn't be any longer as otherwise you can get caught up in them. Suits which are coloured, or made of silk or similar materials, aren't allowed in karate competitions.

You should wear your suit so that the trousers are tied round your waist with a cotton drawstring. The jacket goes over the top with the left lapel over the right one.

No protection may be worn in competition, except a box for men

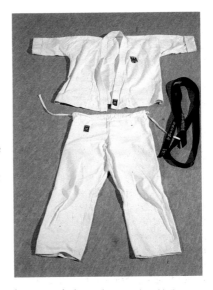

*Japanese gi (jacket and trousers) and belt*

and a chest protector for women. It is therefore best not to use any other type of protection in training either.

Remember that the most important thing is the use of control and the avoidance of injury through better technique. Replacing bad technique with protective equipment is not the right way.

Glasses are fine when you are training, though you may need to anchor them. In competition they aren't allowed and you should wear contact lenses if you have to.

## *Putting on your belt*

Simply place the centre of the belt on your stomach (1) and take each end once round your body (2). Put the left-hand end over the right (3), wind it round both parts of your belt and knot it over the right-hand-end, which is now on the left (4). The resulting knot should be flat and both ends should be the same length (5).

3

1

4

2

5

## *Safety and health*

Like any other sport, karate has its own set of rules about health and safety which are vitally important. The main rules are these:

Don't wear anything made of metal. Anyone who has ever been hit even lightly in the face by someone wearing a ring will tell you how dangerous this is. Also dangerous, but this time to the person wearing them, are chains, bracelets and earrings. If you have a ring you can't remove, cover it with sticking-plaster.

Just as important is that your fingernails and toenails are cut short. It should also go without saying that you should always have clean hands and feet when you train.

Air your suit well each time you use it, as otherwise it will get smelly and sweat-stained. Every two to three weeks, or every week if you train frequently, wash your suit as well.

If you have anything infectious, such as fungal infections of your foot, take proper precautions to make sure no-one else is infected. Remember, karate is supposed to be fun for other people, not just yourself! It is a golden rule of karate that you respect other people.

## *Exercises and special training*

Exercises are the cornerstone of karate training. Whether it is formal exercise, two-person exercise or special types of exercise such as strength or endurance training, you can't practise karate without exercise. It has three main purposes:

- Putting you in the right frame of mind for training
- Stretching, loosening and flexing your muscles
- Preparing you for particular goals (techniques, strength, stamina).

Don't underestimate the importance of the first point above. Karate pupils come from all sorts of different daily situations. Their job, their circum-stances at home, their frustrations and worries are all things which may distract them from their training. Exercise serves as a deliberate way of gradually focusing your mind on your training, so that you are mentally as well as physically prepared and can get involved in something which has nothing to do with your normal everyday circumstances. At the end of your exercises you should have achieved a high degree of readiness and concentration so that you can practise karate.

The second point is perhaps the main purpose of exercise. If you have been sitting around all day at work, or perhaps working too hard, you are unlikely to be in a fit state to practise karate straight afterwards.

Exercise gets your body turning over like an engine which has gradually been warmed up from cold.

Some of the exercises in common use look positively formidable to the beginner: doing the splits, bending down from the waist to touch the floor, doing press-ups on your fingertips. In exercises like these a great deal depends on the skill of the individual trainer as to whether the beginner makes steady, successful progress.

But the main purpose of ritual exercises is to loosen up by stretching your muscles and limbs. Only if you are loose-limbed will you later be able to turn strength into speed.

The third point above is the responsibility of the effective trainer. If he or she trains people properly, they will understand why they are being asked to do each exercise. All too often incorrect strength training does more harm than good. This book should also give the teacher who has not been specially trained the chance to bring strength training into their pupils' programme of activities.

In conclusion to these general remarks, there are three principles you should always observe:

• You do exercise at the beginning of your training session as a way of getting you gradually prepared for the training itself. So never begin with exercises which are too hard or too strenuous

• Gradually increase the amount of stretching exercises you do, and try not to stop before you have started to work up a sweat

• Don't use up all your reserves of energy in the initial exercises so that you have none left for the rest of the training session. This means leaving strength or endurance training until the end of the session.

The following pages describe four different types of exercises you can do in any training session.

*Doing the splits vertically*

# Ritual exercises

1 Jump on the spot; also try jumping sideways, forward and back (warms up leg muscles)

2 Swivel your hips and cross your legs (helps flexibility of hips)

3 Circle your arms forwards and backwards (warms up shoulder muscles)

7 Touch opposite toes with alternate hands (helps flexibility of lower back)

8 Bend forwards with your legs well apart and reach between your legs, then bend back (helps flexibility of buttocks)

9 Turn from the waist in karate stance, alternately right and left (helps flexibility of buttocks)

13 Do the splits as wide as possible (stretches inner thigh muscles and hips)

14 Sit with legs spread wide, bend sideways (stretches leg and back muscles)

Swing your arms back and forth, first with arms bent and then outstretched (warms up neck and upper back muscles)

Move your head forwards and backwards, sideways, tilting, turning and circling (stretches muscles and helps flexibility of spine)

Bend sideways with your feet well apart (helps flexibility of lower back and buttocks and stretches back muscles)

Take up a karate stance (stretches inner hip muscles)

Bend one knee in wide straddle stance (stretches inner hip and thigh muscles)

Squat down on your heel from a broad straddle stance (stretches leg muscles and hips)

Sit with legs spread wide, bend forwards to put elbows on ground (stretches back and leg muscles)

Sit with legs together, reach for feet with hands (stretches back and leg muscles)

Sit with one leg bent, touch other knee with head (stretches hips)

Sit with knees bent, bring soles of feet together and push knees up and down to floor (stretches hip and leg muscles)

Sit with one leg bent, place both hands on the ground behind the bent leg (stretches hip and back muscles)

Do press-ups on fingertips with legs wide apart, lift hips and bend arms simultaneously so that body is pushed well forward (strengthens forearm muscles, flexes spine)

Do press-ups on palms. Bend arms and move them backwards so that hips are lifted upwards (strengthens arm muscles, flexes spine)

Bend forward and swing knees from side to side (flexes knees)

Bend forward and push knees backwards (stretches tendons of legs)

Karate stance (left and right): high straight kick (warms up and strengthens muscles for particular kicks)

19 Sit back with one leg bent, heel up against the groin and the other leg stretched out straight at right angles to it.

22 Sit with soles of feet touching, lean forward on to outside of foot (stretches side muscles of lower leg)

20 Cross one leg over the other and pull it up with the opposite arm (stretches and flexes hips)

25 Do full splits (or box splits) only after a full warm up and stretches. (This stretches and flexes the hips.)

26 Swivel hips from side to side (flexes hips)

30 High sideways kick (flexes and strengthens leg muscles)

31 High backward kick (flexes and strengthens leg muscles)

# Two-person exercises

Two-person exercises help you improve both your strength and stamina. They also add variety to the more common solitary exercises. Depending on whether you are a beginner or more advanced, you can increase or decrease the number of times you repeat the exercises. Try to ensure that all the different types of muscle are worked on in turn. You should also include a few stretching exercises when you do strengthening exercises: this will create more variety as well as allowing you to recover from the strengthening exercises and make you better prepared for your karate training.

**Note** Many of the exercises below involve one person doing the exercises and the other person helping them. They are described as though it is you, and not your partner, doing the exercises, but of course you should take turns.

## Strengthening thigh and buttock muscles

Stand back to back with your partner with your arms linked. Move down to a position like sitting on a chair, then stand up again. This and the following exercises should be carried out 20 times each provided you are both past the beginner stage.

## Stretching backs of legs and back muscles

Stand facing each other, legs apart. Stretch out your arms and place them on each other's shoulders, bend well forward and push downwards and sideways.

## *Strengthening triceps*

You lie down in the press-up position, and your partner lifts your legs up wheelbarrow fashion by the ankles. To improve the press-ups, place your hands briefly on your back in between each performance of the exercise.

## *Strengthening stomach muscles*

Sit opposite each other, with your feet linked and your hands behind your heads. Do sit-ups together, bending forward almost to touch your knees.

Variation which exercises more of the stomach muscles: As above, but touch each knee with the opposite elbow.

To make this exercise more strenuous, sit close enough together and put your feet on your partner's shoulders, then do sit-ups up to your knees.

### Strengthening biceps

You lie on your back, and your partner straddles you at waist height. Grasp your partner's belt, with your knuckles towards their chest, and pull your body as far upwards as possible remaining as still as you can.

### Strengthening back muscles

Your partner goes down on all fours, and you face them, lying on your stomach. Lift yourself up to clap your hands above their head.

### Stretching backs of legs and back muscles

Sit facing each other with your legs as far apart as possible (do the splits if you can). Put your feet together.

Grip your partner's wrists and pull the top half of their body towards you. Hold this position for 4 to 6 seconds, then change roles.

### Strengthening thigh and buttock muscles

Lie on your back and raise your legs. Your partner stands at your feet facing you, legs slightly apart, then leans forward onto your feet. Now bend and stretch your legs.

### Strengthening triceps and deltoid muscle

Your partner lies on their back, and you do press-ups on their out-stretched arms. Bring your shoulders down to the level of their hands; only you should be doing any work.

### Strengthening stomach muscles

Your partner goes down on all fours. You straddle them, facing backwards, and hook your feet under their thighs. Do sit-ups with your hands behind your head.

### Strengthening calf muscles

Your partner goes down on all fours. You put your hands on their shoulder blades and jump back and forth across their back.

### Strengthening back muscles

You lie on your stomach with your hands behind your head. Your partner kneels across your lower legs. Lift the top half of your body until your hips are off the ground.

### Strengthening stomach and hip muscles; stretching backs of legs

Your partner kneels down; you stand opposite them and lift each leg off the floor and over their head 20 times.

### Stretching for front kick
*mae geri*

Stand face to face. Your partner crouches down, and you put your foot on to their shoulder. They then slowly stand up to their full height and keep your leg fully extended. Hold the position for about ten seconds, then repeat using your other leg.

### Stretching for side kick
*yoko geri*

Stand side by side. Put one foot over your partner's shoulder behind their head and keep your leg straight for about ten seconds. Then repeat the exercise with your other leg.

## Building up strength

Strength is essential if you are to become fast at karate. Although in karate it is not quite as important as in judo, it is a fact that if two people practising karate are equally matched in every respect, except that one is stronger, it is the stronger one who will come out on top. But it is also the case that people who practise sports which serve solely to build up their strength (such as weight-lifters, body-builders and wrestlers) often make fairly heavy going of learning karate because they are lacking in the other skills which karate requires. So it is a question of finding the right balance between strength on one hand, and flexibility and agility on the other.

Your strength is defined as the ability of your muscles to perform work in the face of resistance. There is a difference between dynamic strength, which is directed against fast moving resistance, and static strength, where the resistance is fixed. So strength training is also divided into two types: isotonic for dynamic, and isometric for static.

Leg and buttock muscles

Chest and arm muscles

Stomach muscles
Biceps muscles

Trapezius and deltoid
Triceps muscles

In both types of training the degree of strength in your muscles is determined by how much resistance they meet.

## *Static training*

In static training the resistance is so great that no movement is possible against it.

In static, or isometric training, how successful you are depends very much on how much will power you have. This is what will determine how hard you work. The more you exert yourself, the stronger your muscles will become. The main thing is that each period of exertion should last about eight seconds. Any less time than this and there will be less increase in muscle strength; any more, and it stops being effective, assuming you are working at your maximum effort. Here again, three or four sequences to a session are best. This is also the type of training which will give you the greatest increase in strength.

So why don't all sports people train just using static strength training?

Static training has two major disadvantages. Firstly, it decreases the blood supply to the muscles doing the work. This means that the exercise can't be done for very long, so you can't go on and on doing it to improve your endurance.

The second disadvantage is that if you are training for a particular movement, you can't do the whole movement, but only part of it. So although static training will give you instant results in a way that dynamic strength training won't, for making you stronger it isn't really suitable for movement sports like karate. In this book we have therefore dealt mainly with dynamic strength training.

## *Dynamic training*

In dynamic strength training there is less resistance than in static, and the muscles are therefore free to move. This means that there is less gain in strength. Dynamic training involves moving weights. These should be heavy enough for you only to be able to do each exercise four or five times at maximum effort. Once you have exercised the most important groups of muscles, have a break and then go through exactly the same exercises again, possibly increasing the weights if you feel able to do so. In most cases it won't be until you have done them three or four times that you reach your optimum training performance which will give you the best results.

The best way of working out what weights to use is to find out what is the maximum weight you are normally capable of lifting and then take 80 or 90 percent of this figure.

One particularly good way of training is pyramid training. This means that you start at about 98 percent of the maximum weight. Take a break of one to three minutes, depending on your condition. Then repeat the exercise twice at 95 percent. Take another break, and do the exercise three times at 90 percent. After another break do it four times at 85 percent or five times at 80 percent. If you are a beginner make this your first sequence of exercises and then take a break of anything between three minutes and half an hour. Afterwards repeat the whole sequence two or three times to make a whole session. If you are very fit and experienced, you may be able to repeat each 'pyramid', but in a reverse direction, at the end of each sequence before you take a break between sequences.

Keep an eye on your pulse: it should not exceed 120 beats a minute.

It is important in strength training for karate that you preserve the right ratio between strength training and training in karate techniques. This should be around one to five: in other words, for each hour of strength training you should do about five hours of training in techniques. This will allow you to attain a similar level of co-ordination to that before you started the strength training. If you follow everything above, you will be well on the way to achieving the strength you need to train in karate.

*Pyramid training*

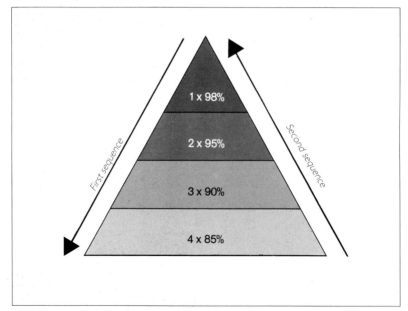

## Strength training with a partner

The following examples of exercises for dynamic strength training are designed for work with two people. Although you won't achieve quite such good results with another person as you would with weights, the fact is that there aren't many karate clubs which have a set of weights.

The amount of effort you put into each exercise should be such that you can't do the exercise more than five times. The closer you get to the right level of exertion, the better will be the results. Do the exercises one by one to strengthen each group of muscles in turn. Take a break of about a minute between each, depending on your condition. After the first sequence, take a break of 3 to 10 minutes, then one of 5 to 15 minutes between subsequent sequences. If you feel up to it, make the second and third sequences more strenuous. These are the exercises:

### Strengthening biceps muscles of thigh, buttock and calf muscles

Work with someone who is about three-quarters of your own height (as in the sequence at right). Put them across your shoulders and bend your knees. Keep your feet shoulder-width apart and the top half of your body as upright as possible.

## Strengthening triceps

With your feet against a wall so that your body is at an angle of 45 degrees to the floor, bend and stretch your arms (see top picture at left). If you are fairly strong make this a steeper angle so your legs are further up the wall.

## Strengthening stomach muscles

Stand facing each other. Put your legs around your partner's waist, raise the top half of your body and then lower it again as in the two lower pictures at left. Your partner shouldn't help you in any way. If you find the exercise too easy (i.e. you can do it more than five times), hold a weight to your chest such as a full hold-all, as here, or a punch-bag.

## *Strengthening back muscles*

Lie on your stomach with your partner sitting on your legs (see picture at right). Lift your body as high as possible off the ground. As in the previous exercise, use a small weight if you wish to make it slightly more strenuous.

## *Strengthening your arm flexor muscles (biceps)*

The simplest way of doing this (assuming you do not have access to parallel bars) is for your partner to stand over you, legs apart, as you lie on your back.

Now grasp your partner's belt with your knuckles facing towards their body and pull your body upwards until your chin reaches their belt. To make this harder, your partner can stand on two boxes or chairs (see lower picture at right), and you can put a weight, such as a bag, on your back. You could also get someone else to press on your shoulders from above.

## Stamina training

Stamina, in the sporting sense, is the ability to exert yourself over a long period of time. It isn't a major feature of karate, but you can't train properly and turn in a good performance in competition unless you have a good level of endurance. So your training should also include endurance sessions.

Apart from simple endurance running, the best method is interval training. This means very short periods of circuit training so that you gradually achieve a higher level of performance.

### When you do interval training, bear the following in mind

Your pulse rate after exertion shouldn't be more than 180 to 190 beats a minute; nor should it be less than 160 a minute.

The break you take after exercise shouldn't be so long that your pulse falls to two-thirds of its rate after exertion: for example, if it was 180 beats a minute after exertion, it shouldn't go down below 120 beats a minute before you begin the next sequence of exercise.

Each sequence should last 15 to 20 seconds, with a break of 10 to 15 seconds between each one. Three to four periods of exertion go to make up one sequence. After the first sequence take a break of one to three minutes. If you find at the beginning of the break that your pulse rate doesn't go down below 140 within a minute, it means that you've exerted yourself too hard and need to take a considerably longer break. You should check this each time you finish a sequence. After the break go through a second and then a third sequence. The graph below shows how the interval method should

*How interval training works*

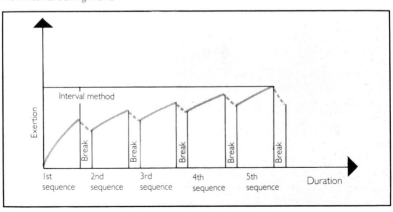

*Measuring pulse rates during a break*

work, and is based on a five-sequence training session.

| Exertion | 15 sec | Pulse 180 | |
|----------|--------|-----------|---|
| Break | 10 sec | Pulse 125 | |
| Exertion | 15 sec | Pulse 180 | |
| Break | 10 sec | Pulse 130 | |
| Exertion | 15 sec | Pulse 185 | First sequence |
| Break | 10 sec | Pulse 135 | |
| Exertion | 15 sec | Pulse 190 | |
| Break | 10 sec | Pulse 140 | |

Break between sequences: 2 minutes
Total session: 3 sequences

The amount of exertion each time will depend on your condition. If you are a child or teenager, or just not taking karate very seriously, running 80 to 100 metres or yards (say three lengths of a 30-metre sports hall) should do. If you are practising karate very competitively, you should be doing 120 metres, or four lengths of the hall. If you aren't sure, then just try different distances until you find what feels right. If you want to make it more strenuous still, try running uphill or carrying weights.

### So to do an interval training session you will need the following

- A stop-watch
- The ability to take your pulse (best either from your wrist or the side of your neck)
- A training plan, which must include the following:
- what type of training you want to do, and what you want to cover
- how long you want each period of exertion to be
- how long breaks are to be
- how many periods of exertion you want
- how long the breaks are to be between sequences

Don't forget also to observe the rule that if your pulse rate is still over 140 after a minute, you must stop doing the exercise straight away. If you do this, you can't go far wrong.

If you have any feverish illnesses, suffer from heart trouble, or have a cold you shouldn't take part in any of these exercises. If in doubt, ask your doctor.

# *Breathing*

Neither breathing nor the idea of *kiai* tend to get covered at any length either in books or in training sessions. But you need a perfect mastery of both if your karate technique is to be perfect as well.

The main rule to follow is this:

Breathe out every time you carry out a karate technique. Of course, if you're doing a rapid sequence of technique you can't breathe in before you do each one. In this case make each lungful of air last for several techniques so that you can take in air after particularly intense techniques.

You should exhale equally through your mouth and nose. Breathe from your diaphragm, not your chest or mouth.

## *The kiai*

The only time you should need to open your mouth is for a special type of breathing, the *kiai*. The *kiai* should be the most powerful form of exhaling in karate. *Ki-ai* means 'harmony of mind and body' and as this suggests it isn't simply breathing out. It has four different but equally important functions:

- Explosive exhalation
  This allows you to breathe out hard when you carry out a particularly powerful technique
- Creating tension in your muscles
  This means you can create the tension you need to carry out forceful techniques
- Concentrating your mind and will
  There is often an obvious difference, especially in beginners, between those techniques which are carried out as an act of will and concentration, and those that aren't
- Taking your opponent by surprise
  Although it may not have a major effect on your opponent, a strong *kiai* can catch them off-guard and have a surprise effect.

In general, the *kiai* is important enough that if you neglect to do it, it suggests your karate technique is not all it could be. In most cases in competition a technique carried out without *kiai* is not regarded as being a proper one.

# *Karate stances*

Asian peoples constantly refer to the idea of preserving a middle way, of achieving perfect equilibrium between mind and body. If you are able to attain this equilibrium, you will be stronger, have faster reactions, and be able to react in an appropriate manner to everything that comes your way in karate.

In karate one of the aspects of this equilibrium is being able to start and end each technique in a strong, balanced and confident stance.

Your body's centre of gravity is just below your navel. The closer this centre of gravity is to the ground, the more stable is your stance. Karate needs a compromise between keeping your stance low and retaining your speed and agility when you move forward or back.

The more secure your stance, the more effective your karate techniques will be. To understand this, you should first understand how a karate punch or kick works. The principle of karate techniques is that you need to attain maximum speed just before the point of impact. When you hit your opponent, your fist or foot turns the kinetic energy it gains as it moves forward into shock waves. As a good technique involves hitting only a small area and not following through, this area is hit hard while areas immediately surrounding it aren't. For example, if you were to punch one tin in a pile of them in a supermarket in the right way, you could make the tin fly backwards without disturbing the rest of the pile.

Of course, the area of your opponent's body which you hit can't detach itself from the rest of their body in the way that the tin is able to. But if your punch or kick is carried out properly, it will be extremely effective. This is partly because when the area you hit recoils, which it does because it can't fly backwards like the tin, the recoil will be absorbed by your fist if it is still there. This is why your fist has to be well out of the way as soon as possible after impact.

There is a simple experiment which will show this:
If you hold up a double page of newspaper by two fingers and punch it in the normal way, with plenty of follow-through, it will simply swing out of the way undamaged. If you do a well-placed karate punch aimed at a point in the middle, the paper will tear where you hit it.

This is why:
Air resistance works against the backward movement of the paper. The comparatively slow, unpractised ordinary punch overcomes this resistance.

A karate punch is very much faster, and the paper has no time to overcome the resistance. It must therefore give way when it is hit, so it tears.

The way you are standing when you deliver this punch determines how effective it will be. The following are the main stances which you will need to be standing in when you carry out the various karate techniques.

# *Opening stances*

## *Attention stance*
*musubi-dachi*

Attention stance is a major part of the etiquette of the karate school. It is adopted when you first come on to the training area and shows that you are ready to submit yourself to the rules of karate. You should bow to your partner or teacher at the beginning of each training session and also when you carry out any of the *katas*, or formal set pieces. Even if you look only at the externals of this stance and not at its inner meaning, the fact the everyone practising karate does it means there is a bond of affinity between them.

## Ready stance · *heiko dachi* or *hachiji dachi*

After you have bowed to your partner assume this stance in readiness for action. It should reflect a state of physical concentration and alertness, with your arms slightly away from your body and your fists clenched.

## Heisoku dachi

This is the same as the ready stance, but with your legs together and your hands by your side.

# Moving stances

There are three main stances used for moving forwards, backwards and to the side:

## Forward stance · *zenkutsu dachi*

This stance is for straight-line attacks or defensive techniques which involve putting pressure on your opponent.

Place one foot about two shoulder widths in front of the other with most of your weight on your bent front leg. Your thighs should not be quite horizontal, and your front foot pointing straight forwards.

Straighten your near leg so that you have the greatest possible forward thrust and when you absorb the recoil you are firmly on the ground. Your toes should be pointed inwards as far as possible without your heel leaving the ground. Bend the top half of your body backwards.

Make sure that when you attack your hips are almost at right angles to your leading leg. If you are using the stance to block an attack turn your hips away at an angle of 45 degrees but don't change the position of your legs or knees.

## Back stance · *kokutsu dachi*

This movement allows you to evade an attack using your hips and the

Forward stance

Back stance from the side

upper half of your body but not your legs, so the distance between you and your partner doesn't increase.

Your near leg absorbs your weight and the backward movement like a spring and then catapults you forward again so you can carry out a technique on your leading leg. Here again your feet should be two shoulder widths apart, with your rear foot at right angles to your front foot. Bend your back leg until your thigh is almost horizontal and your shin is almost vertical.

Partially straighten your front leg until about two-thirds of your weight is on your back leg. Never straighten the front leg fully. At this point your hips should be at a 45-degree angle to your front leg.

## Straddle stance · *kiba dachi*

This stance is used for actions carried out sideways and isn't very common in modern competitive karate. Its main function is to train the calf and thigh muscles and give you a feeling of standing securely.

Plant both feet facing forwards two shoulder-widths apart. Your hips should be dead centre and your knees pushed wide apart so that the lower part of your legs are almost vertical to the ground. Push your hips forward until they are in line with your feet, keeping the top half of your body vertical.

*Back stance from the front*

*Straddle stance*

39

## **Fighting stance** · *jiyu dachi chudan kamae*

It is only possible to outline a general description of the fighting stance. With time you will develop your own fighting stance to suit your tactics and your repertoire of techniques.

What is meant by fighting stance here is the stance used in the *jiyu ippon kumite* and *jiyu kumite*, the sparring techniques you will en-counter later in this book. This is a combination of the forward and back stances. You should be able to use it both in attacking and defending. Your hips should be slightly back, and your weight more or less equally distributed between both legs. Your leading leg gives you balance and firmness on the ground so that you

can defend yourself. Your near leg is slightly bent so that it can propel your hips or your whole body forward rapidly. Your front arm covers the outer side of your body, ie. the same side as your leading shoulder, and is also used to block attacks to your head, and your near arm protects the chest and stomach area of your body, in particular the stomach. Hold both arms so that they can also be used to attack at any time.

There are other possible karate stances, but most of them are used only in special *katas* and have not been covered here.

# **Moving**

When you move from one point to another, your hips should remain at the same height if at all possible. Move your foot to your standing leg and then accelerate from there into the new position. Taking your foot past the leg you are standing on allows you to change your mind at the last moment if necessary. You can either move into a new stance, or add a kick. You should get used to the idea of moving outwards from a central point in any direction.

*Free fighting stance*

40

*Moving forward in forward stance*

*Moving forward in back stance*
*Moving forward in straddle stance*

# *Striking*

In karate there are many different ways of using your hands and feet to attack someone else or to defend yourself. These are the most important examples.

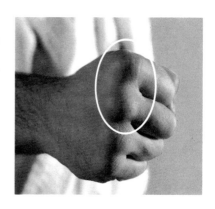

### Back fist · *uraken*
This uses the backs of the knuckles of your index and middle fingers to hit with.

## *The fist*

### Front fist · *seiken*
In this blow you will normally use only the knuckles of your index and middle fingers.

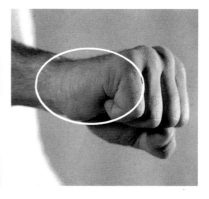

### Hammer fist · *tetsui*
Here it is the outer side of the fists which hit your opponent. This means you need to keep your fingers tightly closed; if there is any space between them it will dilute some of the strength of the punch.

# The hand

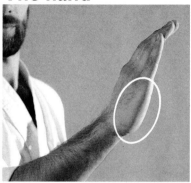

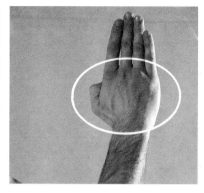

### Knife hand · *shuto*

The knife hand uses the lower out-side edge of the hand to deliver the blow.

### Back hand · *haishu*

You use the whole back of your open hand to attack or block.

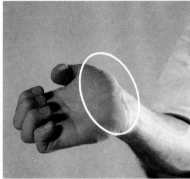

### Ridge hand · *haito*

This is performed using the inner side of your hand, which means your thumb must be tucked in as far as possible out of harm's way. It is the point to the side of the knuckles which makes the contact.

### Palm heel · *taisho*

This uses the heel of your hand to attack or defend with, by pulling your wrists back as far as possible for the strike.

# The foot

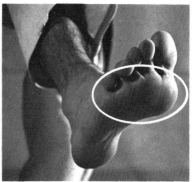

### Spear hand · *nukite*

This strike uses the fingertips in a jab-bing motion. It involves bending the middle finger back slightly and tucking your thumb to the side.

### Ball of the foot · *koshi*

Most kicks are done using the ball of the foot with the toes pulled well back for safety.

# The elbow

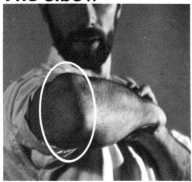

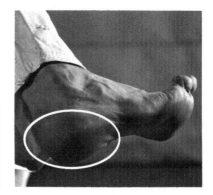

### Elbow strike · *empi*

This is an attacking strike by the elbow from a short distance. It is a particularly effective strike because it is so powerful.

### Outside edge of foot
*sokuto*

In side-kicks, the point of impact is the outside of the foot around the heel.

# *The knee*

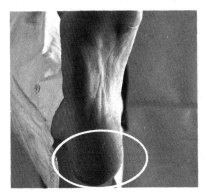

### *Heel* · *kakato*

When you make a strong forward of back kick your heel is used to strike your opponent.

### *Knee-kick* · *hiza*

As with the elbow, the knee can be used only from a short distance, mainly in attacking the stomach. It is also useful as a defensive block.

There are other parts of the body which can be used for striking, but we have omitted them here to avoid going into too much detail.

### *The instep* · *haisoku*

The instep is used to attack the groin or the head. In the latter case it can be used instead of the ball of the foot to kick with.

# *Defence*

*The Shotokan Cup in Budapest*

Bearing in mind the principle that you shouldn't be the first person to attack, defensive techniques are particularly important.

There are three main features of a good defensive block. It should

- Prevent your opponent from attacking successfully
- Make it mentally and physically difficult for your opponent to continue their attack
- Create the right set of circumstances for a counterattack.

To do these, you need to do the following:

- Recognise the moment of attack and the technique which is being used
- Choose the right type of block
- Prepare for it in time
- Stand your ground securely as you carry out your block and tense all your muscles
- Don't carry on blocking after the attack.

To perform all these techniques effectively can take years of intensive training. If you assume that you may repeat a particular block 50 times in an hour, this means perhaps 5,000 repetitions of the technique in a year.

If you reach an advanced stage after three years or so, you may have carried out this block 15,000 times. This is one of the secrets of karate. Not until you have practised a technique many, many times can you reach the incredible level of confidence and speed that is the mark of the expert *karateka*.

Normally, for each different type of attack there is an ideal defence. Which one this is depends not only on the type of attack, but also your situation as a defender at the time of the attack. In basic training, all the blocks are classified according to which attack they are most suitable to use against.

# Single-arm blocks

## Upper block · age uke

This block is used to counter an attack to your head. It begins with moving your fist from your waist diagonally across your chest to reach the middle of your body at about chin height.

From your chin, rotate your forearm rapidly outwards so that at the end of the movement your little finger edge is uppermost. Your elbow should be high and your forearm sloping slightly upwards. Your fist should be about two fist widths from your forehead. Direct your upper arm straight ahead so that the pressure of the attack works directly against your body and can be absorbed by it.

Your other, non-blocking arm begins low in front of your body. At

*1*

*2*

*3*

the beginning of the block this arm
reaches forcefully upwards and outwards, then meets the blocking arm
at about chin height as it withdraws
and is pulled back towards your
waist. As you do so, turn your hand
so that the inside is pointing upwards
and pressed firmly into your waist.
This act of pulling it back gives your
blocking arm extra forward momentum and creates the tension for you
to counter-attack (see pictures on
these two pages).

*1*     *2*         *3*

## Important

- Your fist must have reached the centre of your body by the time it gets to chin height, as otherwise you may block too high
- Your blocking arm should go up outside your non-blocking arm
- As you perform the block, push your shoulders and hips forwards to make the point of impact of the attack smaller and make your block more stable
- Keep your fist tightly clenched so that your forearm muscles act as a shock absorber.

## Common mistakes

- Elbow too low
  Result: side of body not covered
- Fist too close to head
  Result: attack gets past block.

## Practising the block

- First practise standing still and in two stages
  Stage 1: cross in front of chin
  Stage 2: block
- Then carry out the block as a single movement while advancing.

### Cross-body block to inside • *soto ude uke*

Attacks against the area between your neck and your waist are blocked to the side by the shortest route.

The training version of the block begins with a swing. Lift your fist from your hips to a point by the side of your head at about eye level. Turn the inner side of your fist outwards so your thumb is pointing forwards.

1

2

3

*1*                    *2*                              *3*

Your upper arm should be horizontal and your forearm vertical (see top picture on opposite page).

From this position move your fist straight in to the blocking position in front of your body so that the inside of your fist and the front of your body are in line, parallel with the line made by the elbow and the back of your body. Make sure your forearm and upper arm are at right angles to each other and your fist is at shoulder height. Then move forward, either in a semi-circular motion or a straight line, depending on whether you want to deflect the attack or to break it (see sequences at left and above).

As you swing, stretch your other arm straight forwards so that you can pull it sharply backwards as you do the block.

**Important**
- As you do the block tilt your arm slightly forwards and make your wrist the point of impact
- It is vital that you stop the movement at the end of your reach, or you will make yourself vulnerable or lose your balance
- Moving your hips properly is also essential for a strong block. Turn your hips quickly and then stop them just as quickly

*Wrong: stomach isn't covered*

*Wrong: block shouldn't use elbow*

## Common mistakes

- Fist too close to body or too far away
  Result: block not strong enough
- Blocking with muscles at elbow
  Result: attack not deflected far enough.

## Practising the block

- First practise the block standing still in two stages
  Stage 1: swing
  Stage 2: block
- Then practise in two stages as you move forwards
  Either
  Stage 1: foot to middle, swing
  Stage 2: place foot forwards, block
  or
  Stage 1: take a whole step forwards and swing
  Stage 2: block standing still

## Cross-body block to outside · *uchi ude uke*

If your opponent attacks between your neck and waist from outside or you need to deflect an attack inwards, use this block. Swing the blocking arm from well below the other arm with your thumb towards your body. Swing your upper arm to the end of your reach and stop abruptly. This gives your forearm acceleration as it heads off the attack.

*1*

*2*

*3*

1

2

3

The final position is the same as for *soto uke* but on the outer side of your body. Again, the sudden stop at the end of the movement is very important.

Your other outstretched arm should be jerked backwards as in *soto ude uke* and used to give more power to your hips.

**Important**
- Create a whiplash effect by stopping your elbow very abruptly
- The longer the swing, the stronger your block will be.

## Common mistakes

- Elbow stopping too early and too slowly
  Result: block not strong enough
- Angle of block too wide and open
  Result: block misses attack
- Counter-swing by other arm too short
  Result: hip technique not strong enough.

## Practising the block

- Practise in the same sequence as *soto ude uke*
- Also try the block at 45 degrees to the front.

## **Lower block** · *gedan uke gedan barai*

This block is used primarily against kicks, but also against punches towards the lower part of your body. Swing the blocking arm over the opposite shoulder with your thumb uppermost. Accelerate your upper arm first and stop it suddenly on the outer side; your forearm will follow in a whiplash movement. Stop your arm so that the fist is its own width ahead

*1*

*2*

*3*

*1*  *2*  *3*

of your knee and twice the width above it. The back of your fist faces outwards.

As in all types of block, your body should be turned through 45 degrees: this is known as *hanmi*. The non-blocking arm should be diagonal in front of your body and at about 45 degrees to the horizontal before you quickly pull it back to your hips.

**Important**
- Don't stretch the blocking arm out fully or your elbow may get injured
- As you stop the block, pull your hips backwards.

## Common mistakes

- Swing too short
  Result: block not strong enough
- Leaning top half of body forwards
  Result: block not strong enough.

## Practising the block

- Practise in the same way as *soto ude uke*
- Only practise foot blocks with your body turned to one side

As the lower block can often cause injuries to people's shinbones and toes in training if they block without turning to the side, the two blocks described below are best for defending against kicks. In practice one block is very hard to tell from another. The main difference lies in how the arms are used in each one.

*Hook block*

## *Hook block* · *kake uke*

This uses the outside of the forearm
to block from the outside in. Your
thumb is towards your stomach. As it
is hard to swing very far, the block
will work only if you twist your body
hard at the same time, ideally in the
straddle stance. So that the attack
can't continue on to your head, bend
your elbow until your forearm is
pointing almost straight down.

### Important
- Bend your elbow until your
  forearm is almost vertical
- Twist your hips into the straddle
  stance.

### *Common mistakes*

- Raising hips on turn to side
  Result: opponent can attack top
  half of body instead.

### *Practising the block*

- Begin from the standing position
  with one leg in a half circle. Do the
  block in a retreating position.

Sweeping block

Right, above: Knife block

## *Sweeping block* · *nagashi uke*

This form of block is rather easier. Like the hook block, it is done from the outside in, but here it is the inside of the forearm which acts as a block. There is not a large swing, so good work by the hips is particularly important. To avoid leading the attack upwards, turn away and follow through strongly with the shoulder of your blocking arm.

### Important
- Press your blocking shoulder inwards.

### Common mistakes

- Bending elbow
  Result: attack led upwards
- No strong power behind arm from rest of body
  Result: arm on its own not strong enough to carry out block.

### Practising the block

- Practise the block standing still
- Try it against a front kick attack with both partners facing slightly to the right or left.

## Knife block · shuto uke

The knife block uses the side of your hand to block the attack. It serves partly to give you the chance to break the attacking arm, and it also allows you to prepare to grasp the arm. It is not as strong as a defence using your fists.

1

2

3

*1*　　　　　　　*2*　　　　　　　*3*

The knife block begins with reaching well behind your head over the opposite shoulder with the flat of your hand pointing towards your head and your elbow in front of your chin. The defence makes use of the whiplash effect, whereby your upper arm moves very quickly to the outside. This accelerates your forearm as it follows your elbow. At the last minute twist the side of your hand. This gives an additional snap effect.

As you stop your hand, elbow, shoulder, hips and the outer edge of your feet should be in a single vertical plane. Your non-blocking hand is first stretched out, palm downwards, and then pulled back to your solar plexus. Here it stops abruptly, palm upwards.

## Common mistakes

- Turning side of hand outwards too early

**Important**
- Don't move your elbow away from your body, or the block will be too weak
- Bring your hand well up behind your head.

Result: no shock effect
- Stretching arm out too level
  Result: no strength to block
- Withdrawing back hand too far
  Result: your solar plexus undefended and distance too great to carry out a counter-attack.

## Practising the block

- Practise standing still; the hip side of the withdrawing hand should move back. This allows you to perform the block properly in front of your body.

## Knife block · *tate shuto uke*

This is a variation of the knife block in which your arm is fully outstretched at the end of the movement. The blocking effect is achieved by making sure the side of your hand is pointing vertically. It isn't as strong as the knife block and is best used as a safety reserve when you have already turned adequately.

## Open-hand sweeping block · *te nagashi uke*

Here the attack is deflected past its target (usually the head) using the open palms of the hand. Usually a counter-attack is carried out at the same time because the attacker is too busy with the attack to block your own counter-attack. This technique requires extremely good timing and you are only likely to be able to do it properly if you have reached a very advanced stage in karate.

**Important**
- This technique is used to deflect an attack, not block it.

*Blocking with an open-hand sweeping block and counter-attacking at the same time*

# *Double-arm blocks*

In some situations you will need to use both hands to block with. This may be necessary if you are being attacked very strongly, or if you can't turn your body any further away from it.

Normally the single-arm block, which allows you to get ready for a counter-attack, is always preferable to the double-arm block. The double-arm block is therefore the exception rather than the rule.

## *Cross-hand block* · *juji uke*

This technique involves blocking your opponent's attack with crossed arms. Your hands can either be open or closed; thrust your arms forwards from the hips to the point where they are to cross. If both arms are on the same side because of the last technique you carried out, begin the block from that side. Here the arms are placed so that the backs of the wrists are touching each other, as in the picture below.

*Cross-hand block against a very strong attack*

*Augmented sweeping block (see page 65)*

# *Blocking punch* · *uke zuki*

The blocking punch is a special type of block, in which one hand is used to block the attack using a lower block, while the other punches the same point using a vertical punch.

*Blocking punch*

63

## *Augmented cross-body block to outside* · *morote uchi ude uke*

Here, one arm does a normal cross-body block to the outside. The other reaches out forcefully alongside the body and both arms are swung forward simultaneously. While the first arm is carrying out the cross-body block the inner arm is used to support it from the side of the elbow. Turn the supporting arm so that the inner side of your fist is uppermost and your elbow is touching your ribs. The blocking arm is supported by the clenched fist or open hand of the other arm.

*3*  *2*  *1*

## Augmented sweeping block · *morote nagashi uke*

As in the open-hand sweeping block the attack is deflected using an open hand. If you are being attacked with a kick, one hand alone isn't strong enough to defend you, so the other is used to help it. The idea is to lead your opponent far enough forward for them to lose their balance so that your counter-attack is more effective.

### Important
- Your hands must be tense to avoid injuries caused by getting caught up in your opponent's trouser-leg or hitting their leg
- It takes years of practice to time a block perfectly

# Attack

## Punches

The punch is the basis of all karate techniques. Your training will normally begin with the punch, and you will learn to perfect it as long as you practise karate. The punch is the most frequently used karate technique.

Making a fist for karate punches is shown below. Stretch your fingers out, then roll them tightly together so that they touch the fleshy area at the base of your fingers. You may need to learn to do this by doing press-ups on your knuckles.

Next, close your thumb tightly over the top set of knuckles to close your fist. Your fingers and the back of your hand should form a right angle.

*Making a fist for a karate punch*

1

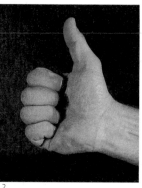

2

3

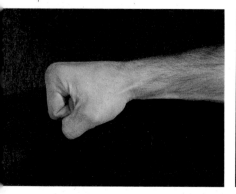

4

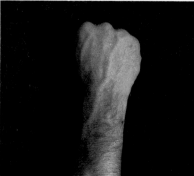

## *Static punch* · *choku zuki*

Before the punch, stretch out your non-punching arm towards your opponent's solar plexus, assuming your opponent to be the same size. The underside of this arm should be turned downwards. The other arm rests on your waist or hips, just above your belt. From this position deliver a straight punch to the target, pulling back your outstretched arm as you do so. To make sure you don't lose momentum by not delivering a straight punch, your punching fist must be kept close against your body as it drives forward. When the outgoing fist passes the other one being drawn in towards the body, they should be beside each other. Your elbows should still be touching your ribs and you have not yet started turning your attacking fist. Not until you have reached this point (i.e. about two-thirds of the way there) should you start to rotate both fists until your leading fist is turned downwards and your rear fist is turned upwards.

This twisting and abrupt stopping of the fist is another of the secrets of karate. Why is the fist turned at the end of the movement?

The purpose of doing this is so that you can punch a point very hard and bring the punch to a very rapid stop. The twist of the fist does this because the braking distance you need is turned into rotary motion. The fist comes to a stop at the predetermined point. Secondly, turning your

forearm at that moment gives you the stability you need to sustain the impact without the risk of injury. This is the only way that punches can be delivered so exceptionally fast and accurately.

The static punch should be delivered so that all the muscles except the ones being used to accelerate the punch (triceps, chest muscles, deltoid) are relaxed during the movement.

Only when your fist comes to its abrupt halt should all your muscles go into intense spasm. In this way the punch can combine the energy obtained from the speed of your fist on impact with that of the weight of your body. The punch therefore resists the recoil like a sledgehammer.

The other fist, moving backwards towards you, is also very important. The action of your fist moving outwards to deliver the punch sets up a reaction in the opposite direction which means you lose some of the strength of the punch. You should therefore pull your other fist backwards just as hard as the punching fist moves towards the target. In this way the two forces cancel each other out and your punch can be delivered at maximum speed.

*The stages of a static punch*

**Important**
- Clench your fist very tightly
- Make sure your forearm and fist are in a straight line
- Move both arms at the same time
- Relax your muscles during the punch, and tense them when your fist stops moving
- Breathe out hard when you punch
- Aim at a point opposite your own solar plexus

## Common mistakes

- Fist not tightly clenched
  Result: punch loses effect or hand injured on impact
- Fist not in line with forearm
  Result: fist bends, and either punch is ineffective or the movement painful
- Punch curved instead of straight
  Result: technique too slow, too weak and so can easily be blocked
- Shoulders raised or pushed forward
  Result: fist has further to go and effect is weaker, impossible to tense muscles as much as necessary, balance lost, increased difficulty in hitting target and likelihood of hitting partner unintentionally
- Fist twisted too early
  Result: fist wanders up and down at end of punch, shock effects lessened, increased risk of injury to

elbow and punch too weak
- Not exhaling with punch
  Result: insufficient tension in upper part of body, so punch is not strong enough

## Practising the punch

- Put both fists by your waist. Move them both forward simultaneously so that they are side by side in front of you. Then move them back to their original position.
- Keep one hand forward and move the other forward and back.
- Both hands move on their own (without the other one) alternately forward and back.
- Move one hand slowly forward as the other moves back, and then vice versa.

*Practising the static punch*

All these different ways of practising the punch are ideal for the beginner.

As soon as you have grasped the idea of twisting the punch and of the two fists counter-balancing each other (which will take something between 10 and 50 practice punches), start doing the movement all in one so that you learn proper co-ordination as soon as possible.

## Lunge punch · *oi zuki*

This punch is usually the first karate technique you will learn as a beginner. Although it looks easy to do, it embodies all the main principles of karate, such as moving in a straight line, having a balanced standing position, the idea of explosiveness, pulling the

punch, and being totally in control of the movement.

Assuming you have learned to move forward in the forward stance and deliver the static punch, now try them together with the lunge punch.

This involves taking one firm step forwards and then delivering the punch using the arm on the same side as the leg which has stepped forward. This means that the large mass and comparatively slow speed of your body combine with the small mass and higher speed of your arm and make the punch uniquely powerful.

To make proper use of this duel effect you should take particular care that your step forward finishes at exactly the same moment as the punching movement of your arm.

*Lunge punch*

As the arm moves at about ten times the speed of a step, you don't perform the punch until the very last moment of your step forward. The lunge punch doesn't achieve its full effect unless your body is totally tense at the moment of impact. The more careful you are to keep your waist at the same height during the step as it was when you were standing still, the more direct, rapid and effective the punch will be. If you move your hips up and down the punch will be weaker and less accurate.

*Lunge punch*

### The impetus for this punch comes from three separate sources. They are

Your back leg, which starts off the movement.

Your leading leg, which becomes the back leg halfway through the movement. This makes you stretch forwards in conjunction with a push from your hips.

The punching movement of your arm.

Even quite experienced *karateka* forget the importance of the second point above, ie. the correct use of the front leg as it changes to become the rear leg.

**Important**

- The punch consists of three flowing movements: back leg, front leg and hips, and punching arm
- Keep your hips low as you lunge forwards
- Punch late, as you complete the lunge
- Make sure your back leg is straight as you complete the lunge, and keep the upper half of your body taut so that you aren't falling forward as you punch

### Common mistakes

- Leaning body forwards at beginning and end of technique
  Result: slower movement, inaccurate impact, and risk, of heads colliding

- Stretching punching shoulder too far forward
  Result: punch can't be brought to an abrupt stop; possibility of losing balance or making excessive contact with your opponent

- Heel of back leg leaving ground during lunge and as it finishes
  Result: leaning too far forward, weak punch, instability on feet and inability to bring punch to an abrupt stop
- Looking downwards
  Result: punch too low and upper half of body falls forwards

## Practising the punch

First, learn static punch and forward stance separately and practise them. There are at least two different ways of learning the lunge punch. Each is done in two stages.

Either
Stage 1: take the first half-step with your feet together; do nothing with your hands yet
Stage 2: take the second half of the step into the new stance, and punch

or
Stage 1: take the whole step, but do nothing with your hands
Stage 2: deliver the punch on its own, standing still

Each method has its own advantages: the first one teaches you how to synchronise the timing of the movement of the lunge and the punch and in the second you can concentrate more on the individual movements and learn not to punch too early. Thus it is advisable to use both methods when you are training.

If you are a beginner, it isn't a good idea to practise the complete lunge punch as one continuous movement. This makes it too easy for mistakes to creep in, and these mistakes can take a lot of time and trouble to eradicate later on.

When you do the lunge punch to the head make sure you don't punch anywhere above your own eye level and remember to keep your hips low.

## Training for advanced karateka

- Use the lunge punch on a partner who is moving backwards and not blocking it. This will teach you how to aim and punch accurately, make you realise the importance of punching fast, and will give you a feel for the large distance over which the lunge punch is delivered.
- Practise the lunge punch while retreating. This will help you achieve perfect co-ordination. It is only when you have learned to punch at exactly the moment you put your back foot down that you will have the feel for what is a proper forward technique.

## **Reverse punch** · *gyaku zuki*

This is called the reverse punch because it uses the fist opposite your leading leg. It is the most effective and most frequently used fighting technique in karate. There are three important principles which govern it:

- You should be defending, not attacking: the reverse punch is normally a counter-technique for the defender
- It needs to be carried out in a strong, well-balanced stance
- Despite this, it can be employed over a surprisingly long distance.

As far as the use of your arms is concerned, the reverse punch is performed in exactly the same way as the static punch. The only major difference is the use of your hips. Normally your hips would be turned through about 45 degrees before the punch.

Here, as your hips have a greater

*The reverse punch being used as a counter-punch to an attack*

mass than your fist, they are twisted back first, and the punch doesn't begin until they are at about right angles to your opponent. The twist should not go more than a couple of inches past a 90-degree turn or you will lose your balance and also have trouble moving your hips towards the target in a straight line.

When the reverse punch is done nowadays, it is the hip-joint of the front leg on which the hips pivot as they move forwards. Bend your front knee slightly forwards to give yourself more forward reach and a more balanced stance. It is the back leg which gives the main momentum to the whole movement. The ideal finishing stance involves the heel of your back leg being firmly on the ground, which helps you absorb the recoil. However, in modern karate competitions the speed and the length of the technique is often more important (especially when the punch is being used as an attacking technique), so it is acceptable to lift this heel off the ground slightly. Which-

ever you do, make sure it is still in contact with the ground.

When you move your punching shoulder forwards you need to compromise between giving yourself the maximum reach for the punch and keeping your lower back muscles firm. The further your shoulder goes past a right angle to your hips, the less stable the relationship between it and your upper body will be. Ideally, your shoulder should be angled forwards at no more than 45 degrees.

If you combine all the movements described here you will produce a screwing movement which, if you bring your hips forward and down will give you a very explosive but compact punch in the static position.

You can also give yourself a little extra reach by moving your front foot slightly forward at the moment you deliver the punch.

*Wrong* (1)

*Wrong* (2)

*Wrong* (3)

## Important

- The reverse punch is a deep forward movement
- If you don't turn far enough your punch will lack strength. If you turn too far, the punch will also be weak because there is less focus to the energy
- The main energy for the punch comes from moving your hips properly
- If you are training with someone else, your fist should be at least a fist's width below your own shoulder height as you do the punch. Otherwise the direction in which your arm delivers the punch and the direction in which you want to direct your strength towards your opponent will be too far apart. What height you hit your opponent at depends on the depth of your stance.

## *Common mistakes*

- Not keeping trunk upright (see 1 above)
  Result: less balance, and therefore inability to carry out movement forcefully
- Raising shoulder on delivery of punch (2)
  Result: punch not head-on and loses in energy
- Keeping hips still or moving them backwards on punch (3)
  Result: main force of punch is lost so falls short and weak
- Raising heel off ground
  Result: recoil not absorbed and punch less hard, nothing to stop body turning too far and tipping over
- Not withdrawing non-punching hand fast enough
  Result: power behind punch comes from arm muscles and it is not hard enough

## *Practising the punch*

- Even as a beginner you should be practising this punch as early as after your first two or three hours of training if you have learned the advancing forward stance and static punch. The reverse punch allows a much stronger forward thrust than the static punch. As in the static punch you should be punching at exactly the same time as your foot comes down

- Also at an early stage you should be starting to learn how to aim the punch and judge the right distance by training with a partner

- If you are training in pairs, make sure your fist is no more than a fist's width below your own shoulder height as you punch. Otherwise you will find yourself punching in a different direction from where you intended. The height at which you hit your partner is determined by your stance, not by your arm.

## *Training for advanced karateka*

- One of you does a reverse punch to the head and the other does one to the upper body

- Practise the reverse punch as you slide forward, without changing feet. This is good training to give you more reach and to move well forward

- If you are orange belt or above, it is important to practise not only punching and stopping the punch, but also moving back in the fighting stance as part of the same exercise

- If you combine this with the spring punch, it is particularly good training in using your hips and pulling back your non-punching arm.

- Used in combination with kicking techniques, the reverse punch will help you learn to keep your hips low throughout the movement.

*Below, left: Wrong – too low*
*Below: Correct*

# *Triple punch* · *sanbon zuki*

The triple punch is a combination of three punches. It begins with a lunge punch, usually aimed at your opponent's head, followed by a static reverse punch to the mid-section, and then by a snap punch, also static and to the mid-section.

The most importance feature of this technique is that it combines all the three main punches. If you get one of the punches wrong, the following ones won't work either, so you can't perform a good combination of all three unless each of the punches is done strongly and accurately. The triple punch is used in examinations from orange to black belt stage, and it is a very good indicator of how much progress the student has made.

It is important not to overdo the movement of your hips in either the lunge or the snap punch. However, in all three punches you should make very definite use of your hips.

## Important

• In the lunge punch concentrate on doing a single advancing punch. If you spend too much time thinking about the following static punches, there won't be enough forward movement in your first one. Because there is a very strong forward momentum in the lunge punch there should be a slightly longer interval before the second punch. This one, the reverse punch, should make powerful use of your hips, but stopped and withdrawn so quickly that you hardly see the fist in the outstretched stage. As you pull back, deliver the third punch, the snap punch. This is again abruptly stopped
• Do all three punches straight forward from the centre of your body
• Don't move your hips up or down

## *Common mistakes*

• Not stopping the first punch abruptly or quickly enough
  Result: weak, unfocussed punch; arm swinging around
• No push from hips in reverse punch, possibly because technique performed too hastily
  Result: arms swing with no force behind them

- Lifting shoulder on punch
  Result: weak, inaccurate punch and loss of momentum.

mid-section, so that your punches hit them dead-centre and at the right height.

## Practising the punches

- First practise the sequence in two stages
  Stage 1: Lunge punch on its own
  Stage 2: Reverse and snap punches
  Make sure the lunge punch is a strong one and you don't move your hips too quickly
- Your partner uses their hands to mark the two targets, the head and

## Training for advanced karateka

- Do the triple punch against a re-treating partner. Aim the lunge punch to the head towards your opponent's chin and stop about 4 inches away. Aim the two body punches at the solar plexus with slight contact.

## Spring punch · *kizami zuki*

This is the shortest type of punch. It takes considerable karate experience to be able to do it, and it has the effect of taking your opponent completely by surprise because there is no swing into it. It uses a strong forward push from the hips to achieve momentum, and your foot also moves if the target is sufficiently far away. Although a strong forward push of the shoulders was once taught, it isn't common any more because it gives you less control over your punch. The snap punch is mainly suited to situations where you are very close to your opponent or in techniques which move into the opponent's attacking movement.

*Spring punch*

### Important

- Your fist must take the shortest route from your centre of gravity to the target
- Use your shoulder and hips only as much as you need to give you strong forward momentum: don't push them forward too far
- As there is no swing involved, the non-punching hand becomes especially important and you should pull it back very quickly indeed.

## Common mistakes

- Fist not going forward in a straight line

Result: technique swings around too much and is inaccurate
- Top half of body tipping forwards
Result: inability to stop punch properly and possibility of excessive contact and/or injuring your partner
- Hips raised and body lifted upwards
Result: punch loses strength and accuracy.

## Practising the punch

- Begin with a fighting stance and aim the spring punch at a moving target heldp by your partner, such as a hand or a pencil, as fast as you possibly can.

## Training for advanced karateka

- Stand about 12 feet away from your partner. Get someone to count to three and move together on the count. On the count of three, both do a spring punch to the head
- Then do the above technique without counting.

# Strikes

Unlike karate punches, strikes are not delivered in a straight line from your body to the target. Instead, they move in an arc centred on a particular joint. There are a number of techniques, but the following three are the most common.

*Above and below: Back fist strike*

## Back fist · *uraken/uraken uchi*

The back-fist strike is very important in competitions as a single strike. It has a wide swing and is delivered very fast indeed, usually at the opponent's temple.

The most important feature of this strike is the use of your forearm to achieve a whiplash effect. It is done by swinging back your entire arm.

Then jerk your forearm forwards towards your opponent, whipping out your wrist from the elbow at the same time. This will shorten the radius of your arm and therefore propel your forearm towards its target.

It is essential that you swing the whole of your arm well out and snap your fist out from your elbow. The back fist strike can be delivered either sideways (*yoko uraken,* which is more common in competitions), or from above (*tate uraken* sometimes used in the *katas*).

### Important
• Swing deep, with an emphatic straightening at the elbow
• Don't tighten elbow as there is the danger you may overdo the whiplash action and injure yourself
• Pull your non-punching shoulder hard back to act as a counter-balance for the strike. This will also allow your punching shoulder to come further forward.

## Common mistakes

• Swing not large enough
  Result: strike too short
• Stopping movement too far away from body
  Result: inability to hit any point

acceptable in competition, making attempt futile; lower back muscles play little part in stopping and whiplash movement and strike loses focus.

## *Practising the punch*

• First do the whole movement in slow motion
• Then do the stretching movement slowly to the stop and the back-snap movement quickly. When you can do the snapping movement quickly and painlessly, do the strike at full speed.

## *Training for advanced karateka*

• Do the back-fist strike straight from the cross-body back to inside or sweeping block without abruptly stopping the defence. The defence then serves not as a block but as a deflection ready for the back fist strike

• Combination: from the advancing back fist strike/reverse punch. This combination has the advantage that your opponent will start to cover his head and upper body, thereby making an opening for your fol-low-up reverse punch and may therefore move into the reverse

*Combination of back-fist strike and reverse punch*

punch. Also the twist of the hips in the back fist strike provides the initial tension for the reverse punch so you can do it particularly fast and powerfully.

# Hammer fist · *tettsui uchi*

The hammer fist strike is known mainly from the various *katas*. In some types of karate it is also used as a competition technique. Although it isn't a weak technique, it is the most difficult to put a lot of power into, and it isn't often taught in training. It is mostly used to get out of difficult situations.

Here again, the bigger the initial swing, the greater the strength and speed on impact. It doesn't matter, therefore, whether the hammer fist is done in an arm (as in the *heian sho-dan* kata) or in a high-low movement, as in the *jion* kata.

The strike should be with the little

*Hammer fist*

*Sideways hammer fist*

*Mae empi (straight elbow strike)*

finger side of your clenched fist. Your elbow should be at the same height as your fist as you strike so that you can get as much strength as possible from your buttock muscles and the weight of your body.

**Important**
• Wide swing, fist tightly clenched, elbow at same height as fist on impact.

## *Elbow punch or strike*
### *empi/empi uchi*

It is difficult to describe this blow with the elbow as solely a strike or a punch. The fact that it isn't a straight movement makes it a strike, but its main effect comes from a strong simultaneous movement of the hips which gives it a punch-like quality. Whichever way you look at it, the blow with the elbow is one of the strongest arm techniques.

There are different types, depending on their direction:
*Mae empi* (straight elbow strike)
*Yoko empi* (sideways elbow strike)

*Yoko mawashi empi (sideways curved elbow strike)*

Otoshi empi (vertical elbow strike)

Otoshi empi

Ushiro empi (backwards elbow strike)

Yoko empi (sideways elbow strike)

## *Sideways elbow strike*
*yoko empi*

This is the most common elbow strike; the others are not described in detail here.

One arm is stretched out fully in front of your upper body. This is usually done above the other arm so that you get more impetus from your shoulder. In some situations, for example after close blocks, an underarm swing can be better.

Then move your other arm, sharply bent, quickly across your chest and stop abruptly when it is exactly at shoulder height. Your elbow should be just in front of your shoulder-line: if you allow it to carry on swinging round your shoulder the strike will be weak and inaccurate.

As you do the elbow strike move sideways towards your opponent in a straddle stance. Without this movement of your hips the strike would be too short to reach your opponent effectively.

The forward push from your hips is used in all elbow strike techniques. All of them also involve your fist being moved as close as possible to your shoulder. This increases the focus of the strike.

**Important**
- Pull your arm well back as you begin the attacking movement
- Stop the movement before your elbow has reached the side shoulder axis
- Use the hip movement to help you towards your target.

## Common mistakes

- Swinging in arc past target
- Not tensing arm muscles enough at end of swing
  Result: difficulty in hitting target accurately, and lack of tension on impact.

**Important**
- As in all striking techniques, a long swing is essential if it is to be successful
- Likewise, the technique will work only if your hand is as tense as possible. This will also stop you injuring your hand
- The inward knife hand doesn't become a curved movement until the final stage, but starts off as a punching movement.

# Knife hand · *shuto uchi*

The knife hand, like the back fist strike, uses a whiplash effect in striking the opponent. This time, it is the side of your hand which you strike with. Because it uses only a small surface to strike with, it is particularly useful for accurately hitting smaller points on your opponent's body, such as the carotid artery or adam's apple. It is not seen in competitive karate, but it is still a technique which is central to karate when used in self-defence.

There are two different ways of doing the knife hand: both are explained in the diagrams on the opposite page.

## *Outwards*

Do the same swing as for the knife block. Then, in the final stage, straighten your arm fully to give yourself the best possible reach and swing.

To counter the forward movement of your arm, pull the opposite shoulder and hip back sharply, as in the back fist strike.

## *Inwards*

Start by swinging your arm from a point close to your ear, with the palm of your hand turned outwards and your elbow at or above shoulder height. Move your upper arm quickly forwards. At the mid-point of the movement push your forearm forward with it, straighten your elbow and strike with the side of your hand, palm upwards, in a slightly curved movement.

*The great master of technique, Brennan (right), against Bosovič*

# *Kicks*

Kicking is also a major part of karate. Without a mastery of kicking there is nothing that puts you in a superior position to, say, a boxer. Karate without kicking simply isn't karate. It is kicking which allows you to create a distance between yourself and your opponent, and kicking which allows you to defend yourself against more than one opponent, or somebody carrying a weapon.

There are three main features of good kicking in karate.

- Dealing with an opponent who is a long way from you
- Combining the power of your feet with that of the rest of your body to produce an extremely strong kick
- By using a snapping technique, maintaining perfect control over your movements after an effective kick, despite having carried out a movement which would have put a less experienced person off balance

It is these three factors which in fact make the kick the most important technique in karate.

## Front kick · *mae geri*

In the front kick the back leg is brought from the forward stance up to the knee of the leg taking your weight, then kicks out towards your target and springs back again to the position it started from. It gets its particular strength from a sharp forward movement of your shin and a strong push from your hips at the same time. It will be properly effective only if you co-ordinate both these movements perfectly. Your upper body should also be tensed forward, but not leaning forward. At the same time, you shouldn't lean backwards either, as this would take much of the strength away from the kick. Another thing you need to pay particular attention to is the way you move the kicking leg. If you only bring it up to the horizontal position, and then make the attack, a kick which is supposed to be aimed at your opponent's stomach will go almost straight upwards and be virtually useless.

Once you have learned to raise your knee above the horizontal so that the forward movement of your shin takes it straight into your opponent, you can co-ordinate the upward movement of your shin with the downward movement of your knee into a straight line going upwards to your target.

The downward movement of your knee shouldn't stop until it has reached an area at or above mid-chest height. As soon as you lift your leg past the horizontal position, bend

your foot and take it into the kick with your toes stretched upwards.

There are two different forms of this kick, the upper area front snap kick and the front twist kick. Both are described on the following pages.

## High snap front kick
*mae geri keage*

This is by far the most common type of kick, and in competition it is used almost exclusively. It uses a forward flick of the shin to achieve a whiplash effect. You then pull your foot back immediately after the kick has been focused, which means you regain your balance and control with lightening speed. The height at which you hit your opponent is not the factor which decides whether a kick is snap or thrust.

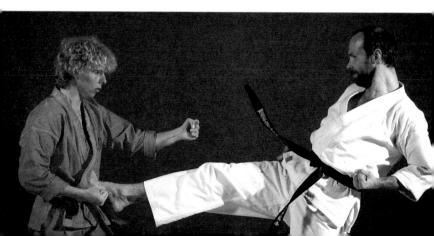

## *Front thrust kick* · *mae geri kekomi*

This kick is particularly strong because it makes even better use of your body weight. The kicking leg moves sharply back just before the kick reaches its target and you can then push your hips hard forward to give it added momentum as it strikes. Unlike in the snap technique, this kick uses your heel to strike with.

*Stopped front kick to the head*

### Important
- Your kicking leg should stay close to the other leg and not swing outwards
- Raise your knee above the horizontal as soon as possible
- Snap your shin, bend your knee forwards and downwards, push out your heel and push forward with your hips at the same time
- Try to keep your body as upright as possible, making sure that your head is pointing towards the target
- The sole of the foot you are standing on shouldn't come off the ground (except for very high kicks).

### *Common mistakes*

- Leaning body too far forwards or backwards
  Result: weak, unfocused, in-accurate kick.

- Not raising knee high enough
  Result: ineffective kick; insufficient focus on impact
- Foot hanging downwards as knee raised
  Result: no tension in kick, and risk of injury
- Swinging arms around
  Result: opponent warned of intentions, kick takes long time to complete because of necessity to recover balance, no time to prepare for next technique
- Ankle joint not flexed enough
  Result: kick brushes past target instead of hitting it straight on (see picture below).

## Practising the kick

- Kick to the stomach (or at stomach level on your opponent's jacket). You should begin practising this very early on in your karate career so that you get the feel for it as soon as

possible. Don't straighten your knee fully. Also try practising it with both of you in the forward stance rather than with the defender in the ready stance so that you can start practising lifting the kick above your opponent's knee straight away.

- If there are three of you, one of you stands in the ready stance as the target, the second kneels in front of the target with their hands on the ground, and the third stands with their left foot right beside the kneeling person and practises the front kick (see below).

*Wrong: upwards 'pedalling' movement*

This teaches the kicker to raise their leg as early and as high as possible, to snap it back and to return it to the ground from a high position.

- Repeat the first exercise but do it twice while advancing. Do the first kick from a standstill, and the second while advancing. Make sure that the second kick is just as high and fast as the first one.

- Do the kick while advancing, in two stages:

  Stage 1: do the kick from a standstill

  Stage 2: bring your foot down forwards.

### Training for advanced karateka

- Stand face to face with a partner and take turns to do a front kick to your opponent's stomach.
- Do the front kick twice: once at a standstill up to the back-snap, and then again from the mid-point onwards.
- Front kick/reverse punch
  This combination means you have to keep your hips low as you do the front kick and then come down low after the kick.

## Side kick · *yoko geri*

The side kick is one of the finest and most effective kicks there is. It is a very forceful kick, but also very difficult to control, and for these reasons it is rarely used in competitions and not highly regarded by judges. However, almost every *kata* includes one.

Again, there are two types of side kick, the high snap and the thrust versions forms. The high snap version is more of a defensive technique used as a sideways block for a strong attack; because it finishes with a fast back-snap it puts you in a good posi-

tion to counter-attack straight away.

The thrust version on the other hand, is an excellent attacking kick. It makes use of the considerable reach that all kicks give, the strength and impetus of the outstretched leg and a twist of the hips to support it.

## High snap side kick
*yoko geri keage*

The side kick is normally begun from the straddle stance. Put your back leg slightly in front of your front one and transfer your weight straight away on to the foot you have just moved.

This is the stance from which both versions of the side kick begin. In the high snap form the foot is moved in a straight line from the ground to the target. It is this straight line which is essential if the kick is to be effective and accurate. This is done by making a compensatory movement with your knee. Without this knee movement (first moving it in front of your body and then straightening it into the kick) the kick will either go too high or turn into a roundhouse kick. When you hit your target, bring your foot sharply back to the knee of the other leg and then return it to the ground. It is the outer side of your foot which should hit the target.

1

2

### Thrust side kick · *yoko geri kekomi*

There are only two differences between this kick and the high snap version. Firstly, your leg kicks harder and more horizontally, so it is drawn back before the actual impact and then catapulted towards its target by your hips. The other difference is that your knee is locked immediately on making contact with the target.

The sideways push from the hips is essential if this kick is to be accurate and powerful.

*3  Final stage of the high snap kick*

*Final stage of the thrust side kick*

*Right: foot rising in a straight line*

*Wrong: foot not in a straight line*

### Important

- Bring your foot up in a straight line (seen from the side) from the ground to the target
- As it is the outside of your foot that you kick with, toes must point sideways and horizontally, or better still tilt slightly downwards.
- The kick won't work properly if you don't use the sideways push of your hips

## Common mistakes

- Knee staying beside body instead of in front of it
  Result: foot swings sideways or from back towards target and kick is impossible
- Stretching toes upwards
  Result: kicking with outside of foot impossible and strength of kick directed upwards, with risk of injury

- Upper body tilting forwards so that feet, buttocks and upper half of body form triangle rather than straight line
  Result: kick weak, loss of balance likely, and difficulty in following with another technique

## Practising the kick

- Practise reaching your leg forward when you exercise: put your leg sideways on your partner's shoulder
- Do the following with a partner: One partner stands normally, arms crossed in front of them, and the other stands beside them. Practise the following: start off in two stages and later merge them into one.
  Stage 1: lift your foot above your partner's crossed arms and lay it down on top of them
  Stage 2: withdraw your foot

Two-person training

Roundhouse kick past a front block

- Do the side kick against a wall and hold it there. You will only be able to keep your foot against the wall if you kick high enough and use your other leg to put pressure on the kicking leg.

### Training for advanced karateka

- Do a high snap-side kick while moving sideways. Before your foot comes back down to the ground, do a side-kick
- Do a side kick from a back stance with your front leg
- To train your side lifting muscles try doing the side kick wearing something heavy on your feet such as ski boots.

## Roundhouse kick
### mawashi geri

The roundhouse kick was actually developed to get round a block by an opponent and still manage to kick them. In other words, if your opponent is blocking from the front, you can still get round the side.

Unlike the front and side kicks this kick is almost always directed at the opponent's head in a competition.

This takes a great deal of agility and is normally done only by experts who have learned to flex their bodies in the required fashion.

*Roundhouse kick with the ball of the foot*

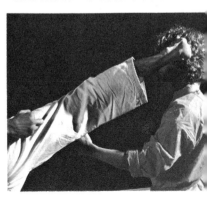

*Training version of roundhouse kick*

There are two different forms of the kick, the first as taught in basic training, and the second as used in competition.

In the training version, the back foot is lifted straight to the hips. Here the knee, shin and foot are in the same horizontal plane and the foot is pointed. Now swivel your entire body forwards on one leg until the knee of your attacking leg is almost on the imaginary line drawn between you and your opponent. Then move your shin sharply forwards from the knee and back again straight away. This gives a whiplash effect similar to that of the back fist strike.

The kick is done with the ball of your foot to the side of the target. As you do so, twist your other foot and heel slightly forwards. Turn it back again when your kicking foot lands. When you bring your leg back smartly you can either bring just your shin back (if you want to combine the kick with another technique such as roundhouse kick/reverse punch, or protect yourself using your outstretched leg), or you can pull your hips back again slightly.

*Final stage of a roundhouse kick to the head*

*Beginning the competition form*

In the competition form first move your foot up to the leg you are standing on or even to the knee before beginning the sideways twist of your hips and the sideways lift of your leg. This has the advantage that your opponent isn't sure until the last moment whether you are about to do a roundhouse kick. If you try it in a competition, but your opponent is able to anticipate it, you are unlikely to score with it.

The other difference in the training form of the kick from the competitive version is that you kick not with the ball of your foot but with the instep (see photo below). This lessens the risk of injury and, if you do it properly, means you can just graze the side of your opponent's hair even if the kick is a very fast one. If you are a beginner, you should use only the training version of the kick during the first couple of years, and even if you are more advanced you should still keep using both forms and use only the training form when practising basic training. This is actually much stronger than the competitive form.

### Important
- Bring your kicking foot up as soon as possible and use the whole of your hips
- The training version of the kick is done with the ball of the foot, not the instep
- Pull your shin back straight away.

*Roundhouse kick with the instep*

*Brennan attacks Mori with a roundhouse kick*

## Common mistakes

- Lifting your leg late
  Result: not enough momentum from turn, and therefore weak kick
- Kicking with instep in training form, or kicking to opponent's midsection
  Result: technique not strong enough, chance of injury
- Twisting body away on kick
  Result: weak, inaccurate kick

*Wrong: upper half of body tilting downwards*

- Not turning heel of standing foot forward
  Result: hips stay back and do not contribute to momentum of kick.

## Practising the kick

- Practise in two stages:
  Either
  Stage 1: kick, and catch the kicking leg with your arm, leaving you standing on one leg
  Stage 2: bring your foot to the ground
  or
  Stage 1: raise your leg to the hip, leaving you standing on one leg
  Stage 2: do a roundhouse kick and bring your foot back down
- Training with another person
  Stand opposite a partner with arms crossed and turned about 45 degrees from you. Start from a ready stance with feet together or a forward stance and do a round-house kick to your opponent's stomach or chest.

## *Training for advanced karateka*

- Two of you stand opposite each other, then each of you does five to ten roundhouse kicks with your leg raised to waist level and aimed at your opponent's stomach, which is turned away from you at 45 degrees.
- Both stand in the forward stance with left legs forward:

  Stage 1: advance as your partner retreats and kick your opponent's shoulder behind their head.

  Stage 2: bring your foot down in the static position
- Do a roundhouse kick from a back stance with your front leg.

*Roundhouse kick: two-person training*

# **Back kick** · *ushiro geri*

This is a very modern kick. It didn't become popular until the 1970s. It involves starting from a front or back stance and kicking with your back leg. If this takes your opponent by surprise, there is very little they can do about blocking it. In competition, however, most back kicks tend to be spotted as you start to turn and your opponent can dodge the kick.

It is very useful for opening up your opponent's cover because, unlike in the front kick for example, your vulnerable toes and shin will not get hit by the block.

The back kick uses a twist of your hips and the top of your body to push you towards your opponent. As you do so, your body weight lowers on to the leg which was in front before.

*Right: Back-kick sequence*

1

2

3

4

5

6

*Back kick*

In the second stage, move the leg which was behind in a straight line from the ground to your target. To achieve this straight line you need to bend your knee slightly and then straighten it explosively into the kick, in the same way as for the front kick.

The back kick tends to be used mainly with a strong abrupt stop at the end. However, you can also snap it back. Strike with your heel and keep your body slightly tilted so as to keep your balance and give plenty of reach to the kick. This also acts as a counter-balance and helps you raise your kicking leg faster.

In the competition version of the back kick you can tilt your body further away or leave it more vertical, depending on how agile you are. But make sure, as in the roundhouse kick, that you use the whole sole of your foot rather than just your heel, or you could get badly hurt.

In training you should try both training and competitive versions of the kick, but keep them separate. Don't start moving your foot down to the ground and continue turning your hips and upper body until you have pulled your kicking leg back.

This is one of the most common mistakes in the back kick. If you carry on turning while you are still doing the kick your back kick will turn into a kind of side kick and probably sweep past your target without hitting it properly.

*Wrong: kicking in the same way as a side kick*

**Important**
- Start the kick as you twist your hips but end it with your hips still
- The kicking movement of your leg should be a front kick in reverse
- Don't carry on turning into your next stance until you have finished the kick.

## Common mistakes

- Trying to do kick in single continuous turning movement
  Result: kick will go past opponent or hit inaccurately and weakly
- Keeping body upright
  Result: without great flexibility, kick will be weak and have poor reach
- Moving front leg inwards at beginning of movement
  Result: turn easier, but warns opponent.

## Practising the kick

- Practise the kick in three stages:
  Stage 1: turning backwards
            Keep your kicking leg behind the other one (seen from your point of view) and turn your gaze towards the target
  Stage 2: do the kick and withdraw your foot to your hips or to the ground
  Stage 3: carry on turning your body and bring your kicking leg to the ground

- Then practise the kick in two stages by combining the first and second stages above.

• Stand in front of a partner with your back to them. Do a back kick from a standstill and bring your leg back again. If doing this in two stages, get your partner to hold your foot to their stomach and if necessary point your toes downwards.

• Try doing the back kick as you advance with attacker and defender both forward at an angle in a forward stance.
Stage 1: your partner takes one step backwards and you deliver a back kick
Stage 2: bring your foot down to the ground.

### Training for advanced karateka

• Practise the back kick as you move backwards, e.g. sliding backwards in a back stance and doing the kick

• If you have limited space to do the kick in, or your opponent comes forward as you do the kick, turn it into a reverse roundhouse kick. Here the kick is done in a curve centred around your front leg. If you make a kicking movement with your shin and sole of your foot, this slightly weaker kick should be quite adequate (see picture below).

*1*

*2*

1

2

3

4

## Turning roundhouse kick
*ura/ushiro mawashi geri*

This kick has only recently become popular through people such as Terry O'Neal, Jürgen Willrodt and myself. It arose as blocking techniques grew more and more effective, forcing the attacker to kick in an arc rather than straight. It is a difficult kick to do unless you have extremely flexible hips and perfect timing. Its aim is to attack your opponent from very close quarters so that your attack goes past the line of defence formed by their arms. This means you can still hit your opponent even if you don't time your kick perfectly. Another advantage of this technique is that, if your attack is successful, you don't offer the defender any room to hit you back.

*Willrodt kicking with reverse roundhouse kick*

The difference between the reverse roundhouse kick and the back roundhouse kick is that in the former neither of your legs moves during the execution of it. The latter, like the back kick, uses a full turn of the body. In competition, use the sole of your foot; the stronger training form uses your heel. There are three main forms of this kick:

## Using the front leg

This technique is the fastest, shortest and cleanest of the three. It usually catches your opponent totally off-guard and gives them no time to deal with your attack. It is best against inexperienced or over-confident opponents.

*Left foot slides forwards*

It is much less likely to be effective against a retreating opponent. If you do try this, jump into it slightly or you won't have enough reach to get to the side of your opponent's head.

## Using the back leg

This is the best-known form of the kick. Lift your back leg high in front of your body, which will make your opponent think you are doing a front or roundhouse kick. The attack from the side with a reverse roundhouse kick will catch them by surprise. Another possibility is to do the kick at the same moment as they are going by in an attack against you.

*Starting as for a front kick*

# Turning roundhouse kick
## ushiro mawashi geri

This kick involves a whole turn of your body, beginning with the same leg movements as for the back kick but then raising your kicking leg to head height to the side of your opponent's head (see left). This is a very difficult technique which requires a very high degree of bodily control. The frequently seen form where the kicking leg is simply swung past the opponent's head after it has moved back out of the way is sheer carelessness and is severely frowned on.

### Important
- This technique requires a very supple body and years of karate practice
- The safety of your opponent is of paramount importance, so the technique needs to be very carefully controlled.

### Common mistakes

- Tipping top half of body on kick
  Result: no tension in kick, and no body-weight behind it
    This means that at best your kick will either just touch your opponent or be out of control. It will also leave you in a weak, unbalanced stance when you have finished the kick.

- Not moving your shin in the knee towards the target
  Result: kick will have no effect and will be easy to block
- Standing too far away from opponent
  Result: leg will not be able to get round opponent's cover.

## Practising the kick

- Practise anything that will make your body more supple
- Practise the whole kick in slow motion
- Practise holding the kick (see below)
- Do the kick and rest your leg on someone else's arm.

## Training for advanced karateka

- Practise the start of the kick so that

*Perfect timing against an attack*

it can't be distinguished from the starts of the *ashi barai, mae geri, mawashi geri* or *ura mawashi geri.*
- Do the kick against a target (either someone's hand or a punchbag)
- Do the technique as part of a slow *randori* to practise the timing.

*Holding the kick*

*Training with a partner*

# *Sparring*

Apart from exercise and basic training in the techniques of karate, you will also be spending a good deal of time practising sparring (*kumite*) with a partner. You will only be able to appreciate the use of pace and the timing of your techniques if you practise using them against other people. There are any number of people who excel at the techniques of karate but who simply can't make proper use of them in competition. Conversely, some people whose techniques and style leave a certain amount to be desired can still score points and win fights. But these cases are the exception rather than the rule: in general the better your techniques, and the better use you make of them, the better your performance in competition will be.

So the purpose of *kumite* is to practise the techniques you learn in training with a view to timing them perfectly and making the best possible use of distance. There are various types of *kumite*, depending on what stage of training you have reached. Each type has different aims.

You should be aware of these aims if you want to make proper use of the *kumite*. They begin with the simplest forms of two-person training, in which every movement you make is decided in advance, and progress gradually to free sparring, where you can use any of the techniques you have learned.

Even though you may have been learning karate for one or two years and have reached the stage where you are competent at *kumite*, you should still be doing the beginner's exercises to put right mistakes or weaknesses you may have. These should be done in exactly the same way, whether you are a beginner or more advanced.

## *Static two-person training*

The first, simplest type of sparring you should try should be with another person, neither of you advancing or retreating. Stand face to face in a ready stance. One of you begins with a straight punch to the head or upper trunk, and the other blocks this with an upper block inward or cross-body block.

There is no reason why you should not be doing this exercise within the first couple of hours of starting to learn karate.

*Upper block training*

*Cross-body block training*

## Aims of the exercise

- Acquiring a basic feel for the timing of an attack and a block, and performing both techniques as safely as possible
- Learning the particular effect of the various blocking techniques.

*Wrong: upper-body movement*

## Common mistakes

- Attacker moving upper body or shoulder
- Not having a clear idea of target of attack and sticking to it
- Not blocking effectively enough.

# Five-step sparring and three-step sparring
## *gohon kumite and sanbon kumite*

Here the attacker stands in forward stance, left side slightly forward, and does a lower block. The defender stands in the ready stance, both arms slightly tensed beside their body.

Normally the defender goes backwards and to the right to block to the left. In any attack, the attacker should stand with their front leg well in, preferably right beside the defender's foot. If they stand in front of the defender's foot, the attacking distance will be too great and the attack will be unsuccessful. If the attacker stands behind the defender's foot, there will be too little distance between them and the attack will be ineffective and potentially dangerous.

Both of you should be careful to keep your legs shoulder width apart (and the defender slightly wider), as otherwise you will lose your balance, your techniques will be weak and you could hurt each other.

As you attack for the last (fourth or fifth) time, do a *kiai* and make it the strongest of your attacks. Your

1

2

3

4

opponent blocks and counter-attacks, again with a *kiai* (see above).

If counter-attacking after an inward cross-body block, the defender should push the attacking arm further away and carry out the counter-attack underneath it. If you are attacking with your feet, it isn't a good idea for your opponent to do a lower block and retreat at the same time. Instead they should so a sweeping block. The lower block and outward cross-body block are useful only when moving sideways, and this doesn't happen in five-step sparring because of the sequence of steps.

## Aims of the exercise

- Using basic techniques while moving
- Keeping exactly the right distance from your opponent even for long kicks

- performing a strong, sustained attack and also knowing how to block such attacks
- Keeping a sound stance even though you are being strongly attacked or blocked
- Attacking each other several times in succession
- Keeping your feet when you are blocking and retreating and setting up a counter-attack at the same time
- Most important, use the training form for your attacks.

*Wrong: defender blocks but doesn't evade attack*

## Common mistakes

- Attack too short or too long, or badly timed (it should come at exactly the same time as you put your foot down from the last technique)
- Leaning forward at attack
- Not having a clear plan of attack: simply moving arm out in direction of attack; blow should land on target if attack isn't blocked
- *Kiai* too little, too late or absent
- Attacker's front foot placed too far outside.

*Right*

## *Basic one-point sparring*
*kihon ippon kumite*

In this *kumite* you perform a strong, sustained attack from a standstill and your opponent uses a variety of techniques against it. Each attack is carried out only once and is concluded every time with a counter-attack following the block.

### *Aims of the exercise*

- Lengthy, strong, accurate attacking from the static position
- Strong defence from a firm ready stance
- Preparing at the same time for a clean, strong counter-attack
- Practising particular combinations of defensive techniques

*Example of basic one-point sparring*

*I*

*2*

*3*

*4*

1

2

*Example of basic one-point sparring*

3

- Stressing the proper pulling of a counter-attack close to the target. The counter-attack must not be pulled too early.
- Stressing the use of hips by separately practising the defence (with hips turned outwards) and counter-attack (hips turned inwards).

## Common mistakes

- Weak attack not devised to take advantage of weaknesses in defence
- Poor stance after blocking
  Result: weak, inaccurate counter-attack
- Giving up basic training techniques in favour of competitive ones
  Result: techniques which are not clear-cut or controlled.

### Free-style one-point sparring · *jiyu ippon kumite*

This *kumite* is like a kind of snapshot of a free sparring session. One stage of the sparring is taken out and practised separately. Both partners begin in fighting stance. Using relaxed, free movements, begin with a carefully-aimed, pre-announced attack. Your opponent blocks this using methods they have learned or which need practice, and then counter-attacks. The counter-attack ends by immediately withdrawing into *kamae*, i.e. in the fighting stance and in a state of awareness of one's opponent (*zanshin*).

### Aims of the exercise

- To cover all aspects of sparring within the framework of an attack. The attacker has to choose the best time and the best distance for the attack.

- Bringing the defender into the most difficult position possible by moving before the attack and by feinting.

- Training defender to judge what kind of attack to expect and when it is going to come, based on the attacker's movements before the attack begins. Because both sides have to think so carefully about what the other is up to, there is a distinctive tension to this *kumite*. If this tension is missing, the situation is an unrealistic one and will not teach either of you anything about the art of free sparring.

- The defender should practise taking up plenty of space and making large, expansive blocking movements. Once they have mastered these, they will also be able to block within a smaller space if they have to.

- The counter-attack should be mainly aimed at your upper trunk, until your opponent has learned to hit your head quickly and easily, without braking too early.

*1*

*2*
*3*

## Common mistakes

- Lack of preparation
  Result: attack delivered from wrong distance or at wrong time.
    One of the main things you should be thinking about before you start the attack is your distance. If your opponent is constantly retreating, you aren't going to be at the best possible distance because they will always tend to be too far away from you. If you get too close as you move into the attack, your opponent can counter directly with a snap punch (see below).
- Defender not getting into upright stable position for block
  Result: counter-attack too weak, inaccurate and possibly dangerous to attacker.

*Counter-attack from a short distance using snap punch*

1

2

3

4

## One-point sparring with follow-up attack · *kaeshi ippon kumite*

The *kaeshi ippon kumite* is based on the assumption that there will be a follow-up to an attack. After the defender has successfully blocked you, they not only have the chance to do a very short counter-attack; they can even take the initiative and attack with a full kick. This means you start in the attacking position, then become the defender and end the *kumite* with a static counter-attack.

### Aims of the exercise

- After you have attacked, you should always be ready to defend. The first defender should learn how to attack while retreating or moving sideways and be able to do so without thinking about it

- The first attacker should feel that the best form of defence against a counter-attack is a very strong attack by themselves
- You should be acquiring a feel for the use of space and creating the right distance which will allow the defender to get out of any situation with an attack that is suited to that situation.

## Common mistakes

- Weak and half-hearted attacks
- Defender moving backwards instead of sideways to avoid attack
- Using techniques inappropriate for circumstances.

*1*

*2*

*3*

*4*

## *Double attack one-point sparring* · *okuri ippon kumite*

In this form of *kumite*, you attack twice. The first time you tell your opponent what you plan to do: the second attack will depend on what happens. This means the defender has to block twice before they can carry out their own counter-attack.

3

1

4

2

5

## Aims of the exercise

• To teach both how to attack and how to react to attacks
• To simulate very closely actual competitive situations.

## Common mistakes

• As for one-point sparring with follow-up attack.

*3*

*1*

*4*

*2*

*5*

'De-Ai', moving into the attack

# **Free sparring**
## *jiyu kumite*

Free sparring represents the culmination of all the two-person exercises you have been practising. It is a long, hard road from your first careful static exercises to a free-moving, non-prearranged attack. If you tread this road carefully, both of you will be in a position to fight well and, above all, safely. There is very little difference between good free-style one-point sparring (*jiyu ippon kumite*) and actual free sparring.

Once you have worked your way through all the stages of free sparring, you will also be a good competitive *karateka*.

The word *kata* is rather difficult to translate. Literally it means something along the lines of form, but its usage is to describe a type of practice fighting against a number of imaginary opponents, and in accordance with pre-set movements. Serving both to help you perfect your karate techniques, and as a test of what you have learned so far, the *katas* combine everything you have learned about karate into one activity.

If you neglect your *kata* training, or simply fail to do it at all, you will become very much a one-sided specialist. You may be good at sparring, but you can never be good at karate as a whole.

Just as karate is more than a series of physical movements, so is karate technique incomplete without the *katas*. Although there isn't enough room to describe them in detail in the space available, you are very strongly advised to learn them and practise them regularly.

# *Afterword*

If you have worked your way through this book, you should have a good basic knowledge of karate. You should know how to exercise and prepare for karate, and you should be familiar with karate techniques and sparring.

There are two things you should bear in mind before you close this book.

## *Firstly –*

karate is something which is complex and consists of a wide variety of elements forming a whole. You can't take any one aspect of karate and look at it in isolation from all the others. This applies not just to your physical, but also to your mental training. So you can't say one minute that you are practising karate, and the next minute that you have finished. If you choose to take up karate you will be judged as a whole person, even though you might prefer to select certain aspects of what you do and be judged on them alone.

## *Secondly –*

karate is a fighting method. If you take up karate, you take on a responsibility as well. You have a responsibility to people you train with, people you compete against and even towards people who might attack you in a real-life situation. Karate makes great demands on your self-discipline and awareness of your responsibilities. If you forget this, whether you are learning or teaching, you are indulging not in karate, but a form of street brawling.

# *Glossary*

The most common Japanese terms in karate

### *Pronunciation*
In general words are pronounced phonetically. There are some exceptions:

Vowels are pure vowels, not lengthened into diphthongs the way they are in English. For example, **o** is always pronounced like the **o** in **pot**, not like the **oa** in **coat.** Combinations of vowels, such as **ae** and **ei** are pronounced as two separate sounds. The **r** sound is a trilled, rolling sound. The **u** sound is usually elided: for example, **oi zuki** becomes **oi s'ki** and **Sumo** becomes **S'mo**.

---

### *Commands*

| | |
|---|---|
| **Yoi** | Ready |
| **Hajime** | Begin! Fight! |
| **Yame!** | Stop! |
| **Mawate!** | Turn! |
| **Mokuzo!** | Concentration/meditation before bowing to partner |
| **Seiza** | Kneel! |
| **Sensei-ni rei!** | Bow to teacher! |
| **Gedan barai kamaete!** | Go into ready stance with gedan barai |

---

### *Areas of the body*

| | |
|---|---|
| **Gedan** | Below the belt |
| **Chudan** | Between the belt and the neck |
| **Jodan** | The head |

## Stances

| | |
|---|---|
| **Shizentai** | Natural stance |
| **Zenkutsu dachi** | Forward stance |
| **Kokutsu dachi** | Back stance |
| **Kiba dachi** | Straddle stance |
| **Hanmi** | Forward stance with hips at 45° |
| **Kamae** | Fighting stance |
| **Hungetsu dachi** | Half-moon stance (tension towards inside) |
| **Sanchin dachi** | Hourglass stance (small stance with tension towards inside) |
| **Sochin dachi** | Power stance<br>Forward stance, but with back knee open and tension towards outside |

## Other expressions

| | |
|---|---|
| **Age** | Raise |
| **Ashi** | Leg |
| **Barai** | Sweep |
| **Dojo** | Where you train, a club |
| **Empi** | Elbow |
| **Fumikomi** | Stamping kick |
| **Hara** | Physical and mental focus |
| **Hidari** | Left |
| **Hiza** | Knee |
| **Ippon** | One point, once |
| **Jiyu** | Free |
| **Kagi zuki** | Hook punch |
| **Kakato** | Heel |
| **Karateka** | Person practising karate |
| **Karategi** | Karate suit |
| **Kata** | Literally, form: training pattern involving fighting against imaginary opponents |
| **Keage** | High snap |
| **Kekomi** | Thrust, thrusting movement |
| **Kiai** | Karate shout |
| **Kihon** | Basic training |
| **Kime** | Focus of tension in the body |

| | |
|---|---|
| **Kumite** | Sparring |
| **Mae** | Straight |
| **Makiwara** | Striking post |
| **Mawashi** | Circular, curved |
| **Migi** | Right |
| **Mikazuki geri** | Crescent kick |
| **Neko ashi dach** | Cat stance |
| **Ren geri** | Alternate kicking |
| **Ren zuki** | Alternate punching |
| **Shiai** | Competition |
| **Tate zuki** | Vertical punch |
| **Tsuki** | Punch |
| **Uchi** | Strike |
| **Uke** | Block |
| **Ura zuki** | Close punch (short-distance punch without twisting the fist) |
| **Ushiro** | Backwards |
| **Yoko** | Sideways |

## *Numbers*

| | |
|---|---|
| **Ichi** | One |
| **Ni** | Two |
| **San** | Three |
| **Shi** | Four |
| **Go** | Five |
| **Roku** | Six |
| **Shichi** | Seven |
| **Hachi** | Eight |
| **Ku** | Nine |
| **Ju** | Ten |